For Mr. Max, who was born on the original Earth Day—J.W.

For my grandfathers, Rusty and Gene—R.N.S.

AUTHOR'S NOTE

On March 22, 1987, a barge called the *Mobro 4000* departed from Islip, a city on New York's Long Island, hauling nearly thirty-two hundred tons of garbage. Thus began one of the strangest sagas in the history of trash—the story of the infamous Garbage Barge.

By the late 1980s, Long Island's landfills were overflowing with garbage and polluting the groundwater. This prompted the local government to outlaw the burying of any more garbage. However, the alternative, hauling garbage upstate, was very expensive. So when Islip was approached by some businessmen with a cheaper choice—shipping the garbage to dumping grounds in the South— this seemed like the Answer to the city's problems. Alas, it turned out not to be the Answer at all, but instead a costly, embarrassing fiasco: a six-month, six-thousand-mile journey for the unsightly Garbage Barge, unwelcome at every port.

This strange-but-true story brought a lot of national attention to the problem of garbage and what to do with it. After the Garbage Barge, recycling—which is far better for the environment than burying garbage—became a much more widely enforced practice. By recycling glass, plastic, paper, and metal, we waste less and help the earth by not stuffing it with so much garbage. And though the city of Islip still produces almost twice as much garbage as the national average, it deals with its refuse more efficiently: thirty-five percent is now recycled, and twenty percent is burned in "waste-to-energy" plants. Progress!

<><

My fictionalized version of the true Garbage Barge story has taken some liberties with the facts. Various real-life characters have been eliminated, and the business partnership has been turned into one invented character, Gino Stroffolino, for the sake of simplicity and, well, humor!

Text copyright © 2010 by Jonah Winter · Illustrations copyright © 2010 by Red Nose Studio · All rights reserved. · Published in the United States by Schwartz & Wade Books, an imprint of Random House Children's Books, a division of Random House, Inc., New York. · Schwartz & Wade Books and the colophon are trademarks of Random House, Inc. · *Library of Congress Cataloging-in-Publication Data* · Winter, Jonah. · Here comes the garbage barge! / Jonah Winter ; illustrated by Red Nose Studio. — 1st ed. · p. cm. · Summary: In the spring of 1987, the town of Islip, New York, with no place for its 3,168 tons of garbage, loads it on a barge that sets out on a 162-day journey along the east coast, around the Gulf of Mexico, down to Belize, and back again, in search of a place willing to accept and dispose of its very smelly cargo. · ISBN 978-0-375-85218-3 (alk. paper) — ISBN 978-0-375-95218-0 (glb : alk. paper) · [1. Refuse and refuse disposal—Fiction. 2. Barges—Fiction. 3. Voyages and travel— Fiction. 4. Islip (N.Y.)—History—20th century—Fiction.] I. Red Nose Studio, ill. II. Title. · PZ7.W75477Her 2010 · [E]—dc22 · 2008040709 The text of this book is set in Filosofia. · The illustrations are hand-built three-dimensional sets shot with a Canon digital SLR camera grafted onto the back of a Horseman 4x5 camera. The line art was drawn with Hunt 108 pen nibs and Higgins waterproof black ink on paper. MANUFACTURED IN MALAYSIA · 10 9 8 7 6 5 4 3 2 1 · First Edition

HERE COMES THE GARBAGE BARGE!

WRITTEN BY
Jonah Winter

ILLUSTRATED BY
Red Nose Studio

schwartz & wade books · new york

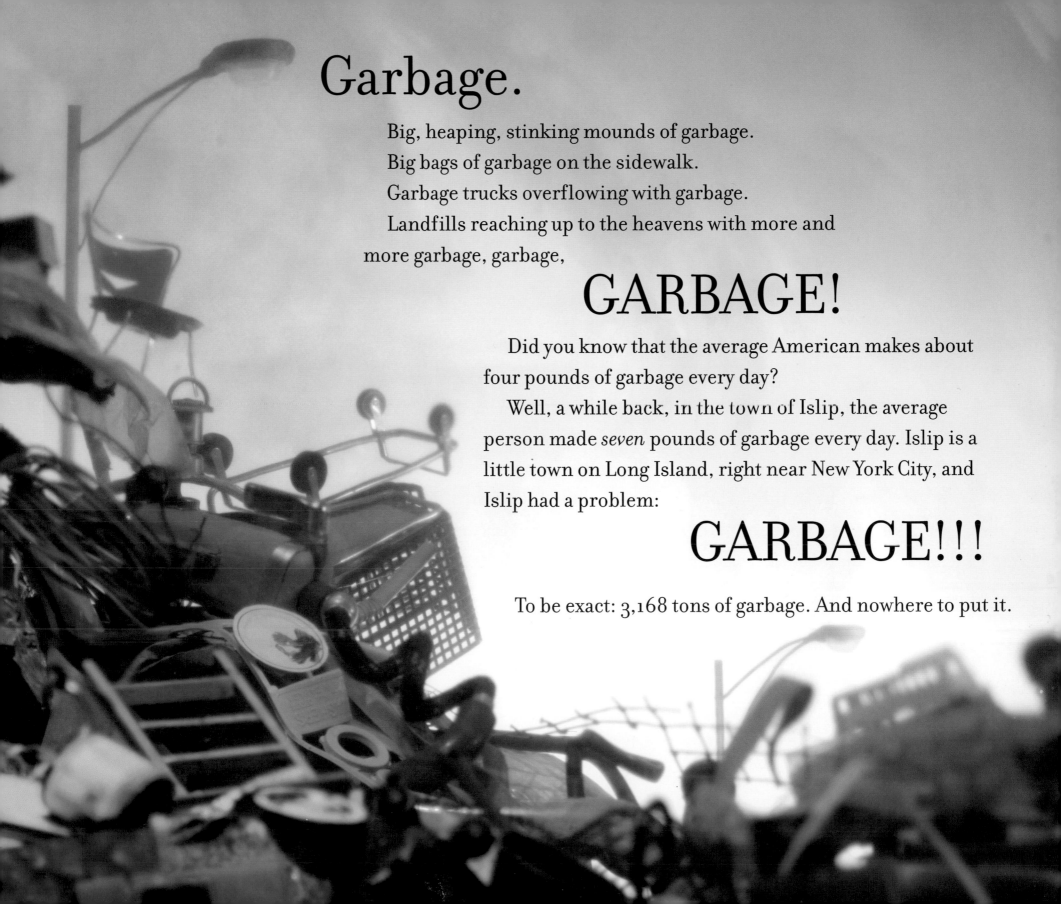

Garbage.

Big, heaping, stinking mounds of garbage.

Big bags of garbage on the sidewalk.

Garbage trucks overflowing with garbage.

Landfills reaching up to the heavens with more and more garbage, garbage,

GARBAGE!

Did you know that the average American makes about four pounds of garbage every day?

Well, a while back, in the town of Islip, the average person made *seven* pounds of garbage every day. Islip is a little town on Long Island, right near New York City, and Islip had a problem:

GARBAGE!!!

To be exact: 3,168 tons of garbage. And nowhere to put it.

Enter the Garbage Barge!

See, this guy in the garbage business named Gino Stroffolino
came up with a brilliant plan: A garbage barge would carry
the Long Island garbage down to North Carolina.

Mr. Stroffolino had a friend there, Joey LaMotta.

"Everyting is arranged," Joey'd told him. "You bring me dat garbage—I'll take care of it."

Some poor farmers would be paid to take the garbage and bury it on their farms.

Clever, huh?

So on March 22, 1987, all 3,168 tons of garbage was loaded up. Then a little tugboat named the *Break of Dawn* began its long journey south, tugging the rusty old Garbage Barge behind it.

The *Break of Dawn* was a happy little tugboat. Her captain *and* crew was Cap'm Duffy St. Pierre, a crusty old sailor. Together they tugged the Garbage Barge down the East Coast of America.

"TOOT TOOT,"

said the tugboat as it entered the harbor at Morehead City, North Carolina.

NORTH CAROLINA

LAND OF SAND DUNES AND PINE TREES, OF BAR-B-QUE
AND MOUNTAINS AND BASKETBALL . . .

Smelling something strange,
two old sisters who lived on the beach ran
and got their binoculars.
"Look!" said Miss Alma McTiver. "It's garbage!"
"In our beautiful harbor?" said Miss Ida McTiver.
"What the hairy heck? That ain't right! Call the law!"

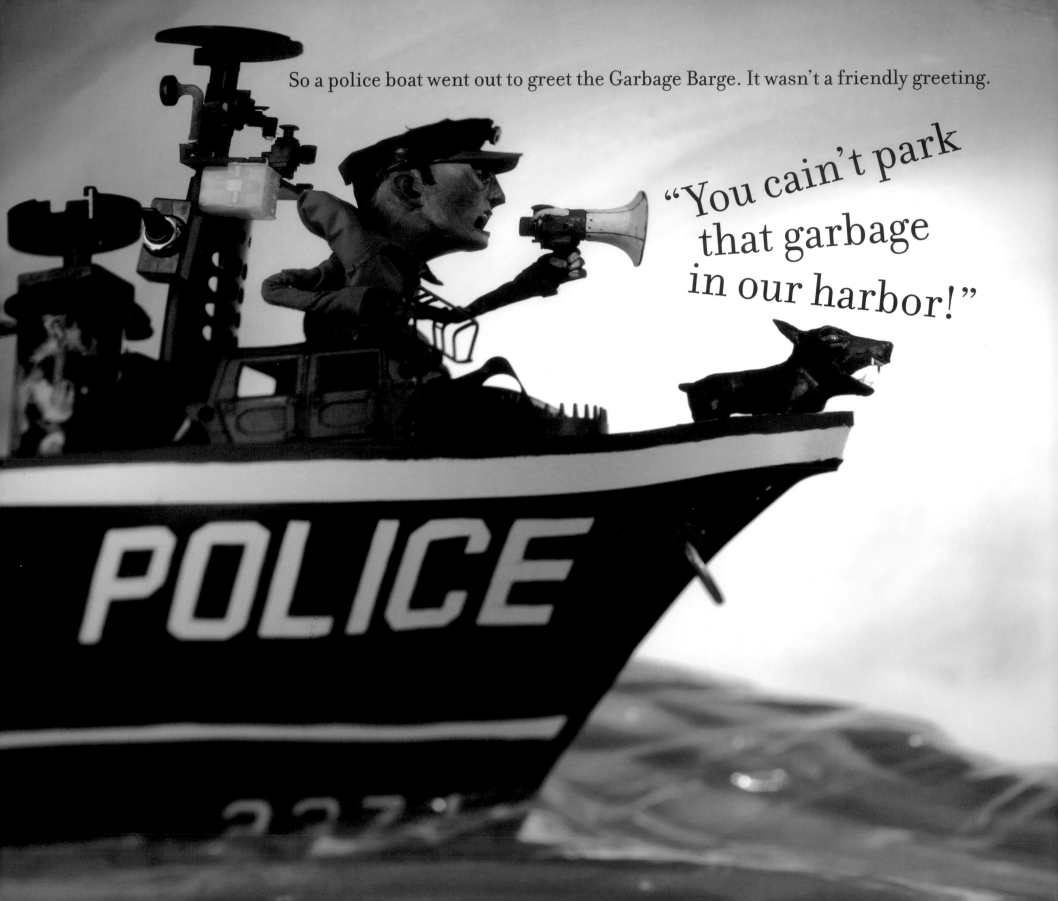

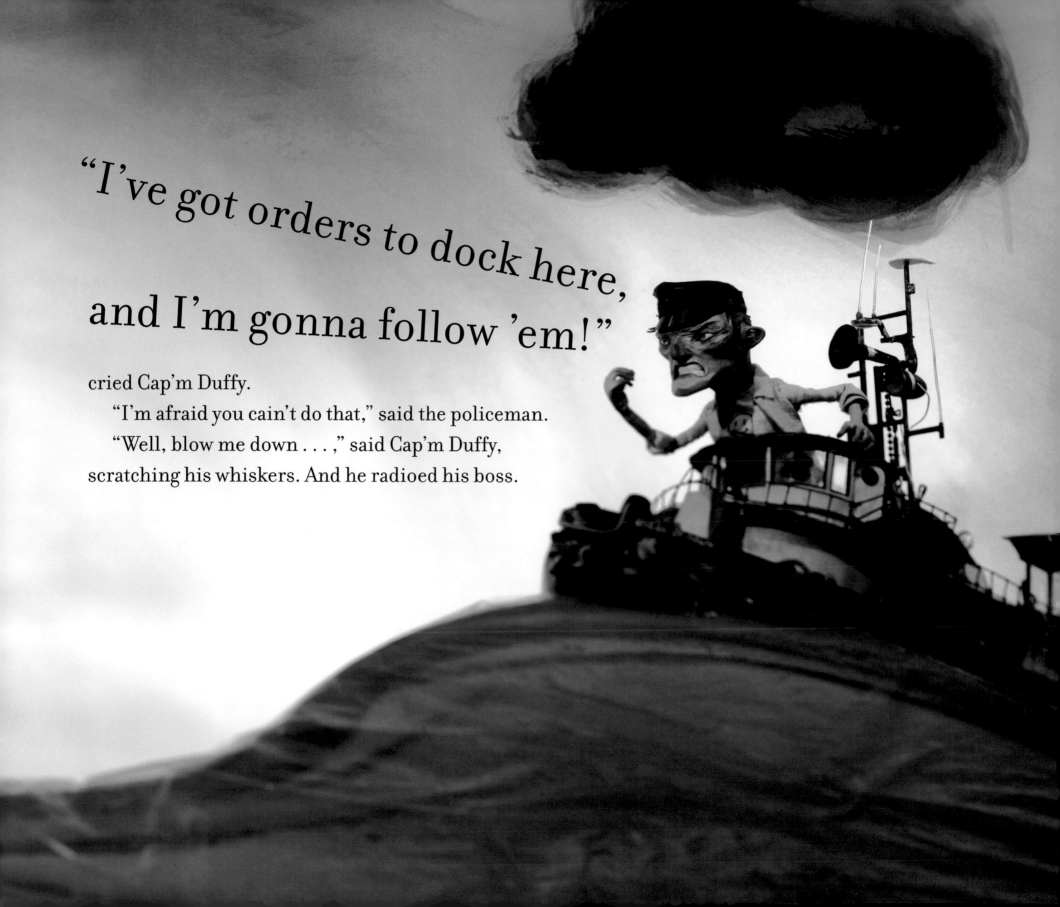

"I've got orders to dock here, and I'm gonna follow 'em!"

cried Cap'm Duffy.

"I'm afraid you cain't do that," said the policeman.

"Well, blow me down . . . ," said Cap'm Duffy, scratching his whiskers. And he radioed his boss.

"They don't want our garbage," Cap'm Duffy said
to Gino Stroffolino. "Where's that fella who was
supposed to meet me?"

"Joey had a little accident," said Mr. Stroffolino.
"Just stay put while I make a coupla calls."

But the minutes turned into hours turned into
days—just Cap'm Duffy with a barge full of
garbage. It wasn't much company.

Finally, Mr. Stroffolino's voice came
through on the radio. "Bring dat garbage
down to New Orleans," he said.

"I know dis guy—Tony Cafone.
He'll take it."

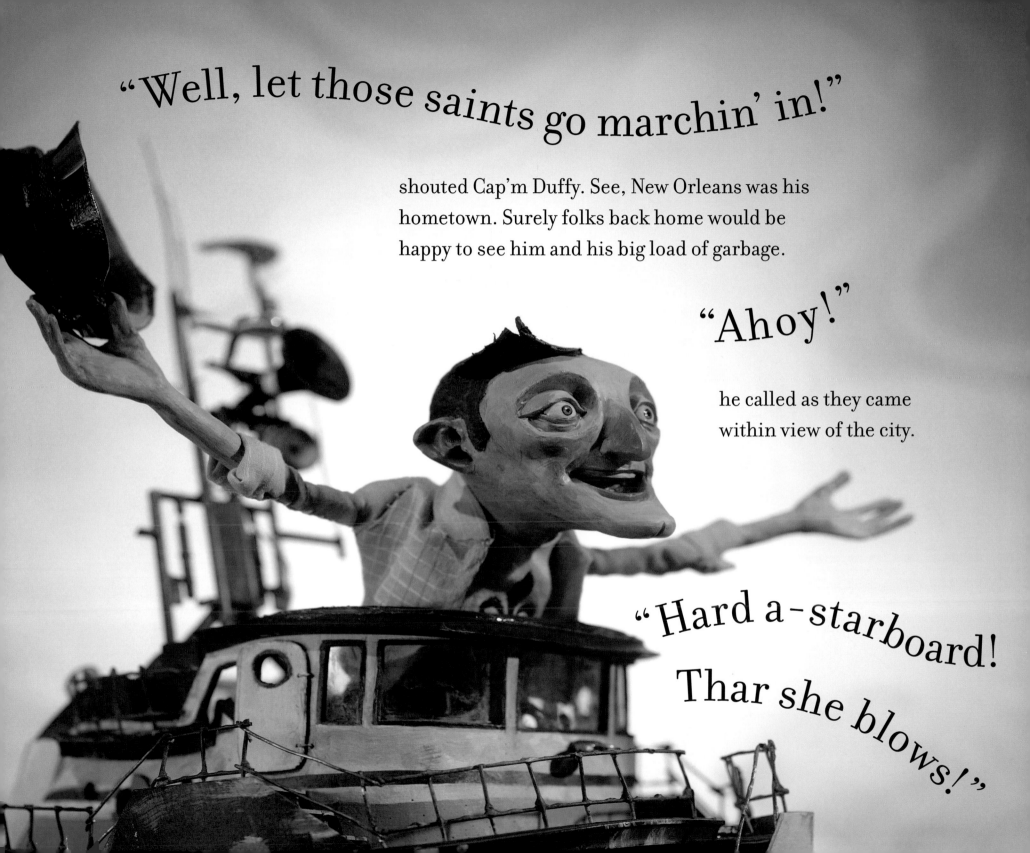

"Well, let those saints go marchin' in!"

shouted Cap'm Duffy. See, New Orleans was his
hometown. Surely folks back home would be
happy to see him and his big load of garbage.

"Ahoy!"

he called as they came
within view of the city.

"Hard a-starboard!
Thar she blows!"

New Orleans

BIRTHPLACE OF JAZZ. HOME OF BLACKENED REDFISH AND STREETS FILLED
WITH MUSIC, FRIENDLY FACES, STREETCARS, GARBAGE . . .

The mayor could see the Garbage Barge way off on the horizon.
News of the wandering garbage had already reached him. "We've got
enough of our own trash," he told his staff. "Call the coast guard!"

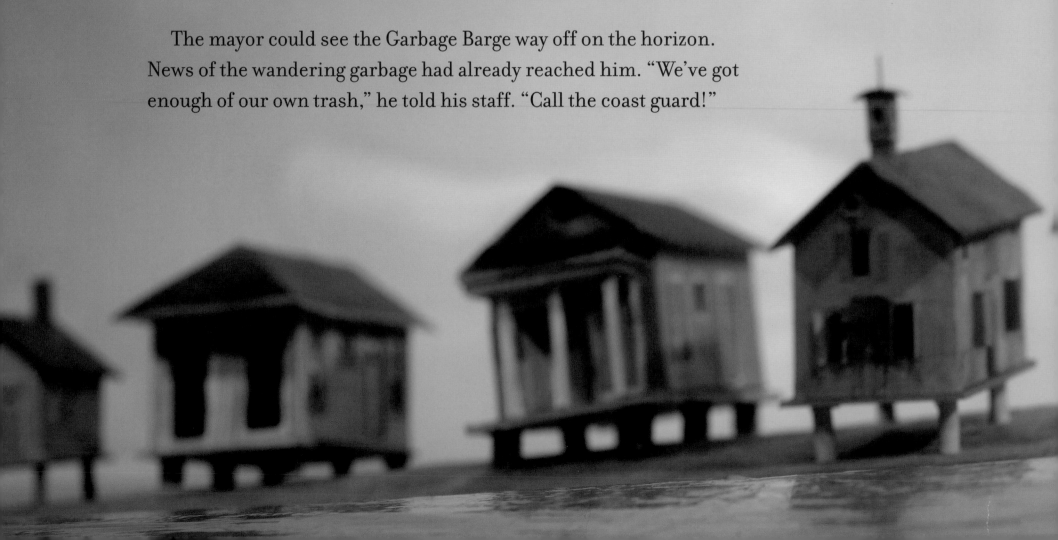

The coast guard arrived just in time to
stop the Garbage Barge from making its way
up the mighty Mississippi.

"Shiver me timbers," moaned Cap'm
Duffy. "You can't do this to a hometown boy!"

"Oh, yes,
we can,"

cried the coast guard.

What could Cap'm Duffy say?
"All righty, then. Full speed backwards!"
he ordered himself.
"Aye-aye, Cap'm," he answered.
And, at dusk, the *Break of Dawn* and the tired old Garbage
Barge began their sad journey back out to sea.

There they were—floating out in the middle of the Gulf of Mexico. This was getting ridiculous. Would no one take this garbage (which, by the way, was really starting to stink)?

Cap'm Duffy radioed his boss.

"Okay," said Gino Stroffolino. "Dere's dis guy down in Mexico—he owes me a favor. Goes by da name of John Smith. I'll tell him you're coming."

"All righty, then," Cap'm Duffy grumbled.

"Southward ho."

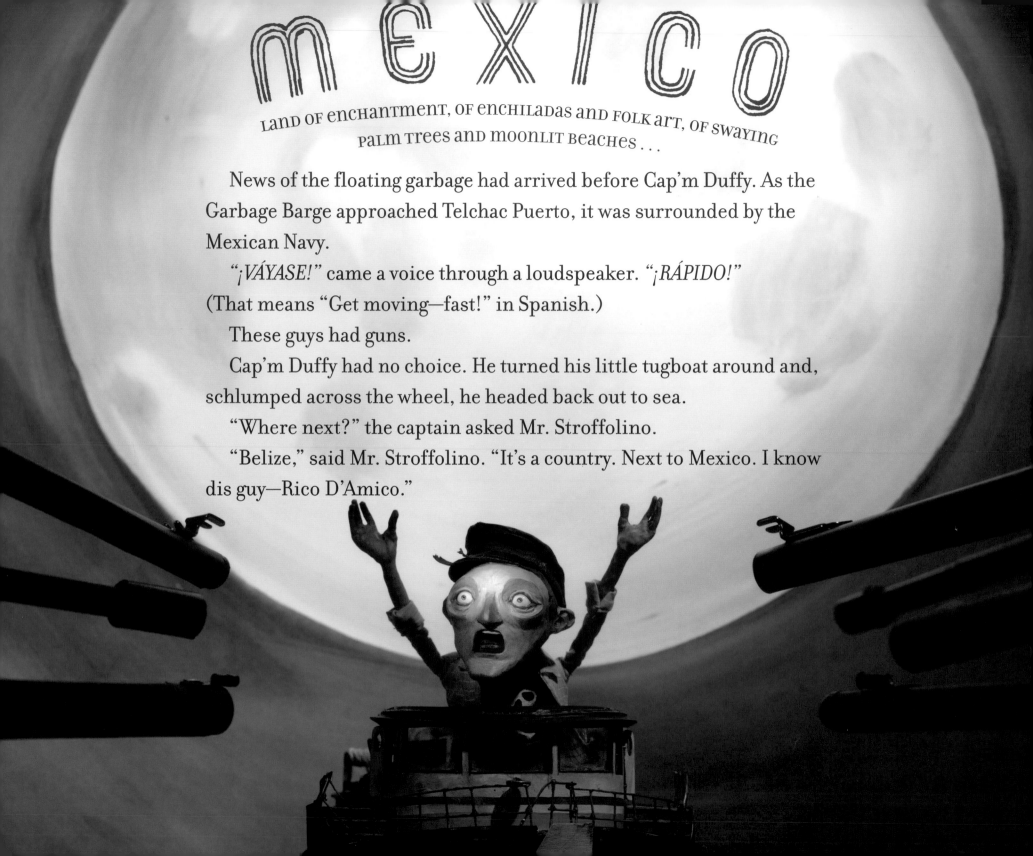

MEXICO

LAND OF ENCHANTMENT, OF ENCHILADAS AND FOLK ART, OF SWAYING PALM TREES AND MOONLIT BEACHES . . .

News of the floating garbage had arrived before Cap'm Duffy. As the Garbage Barge approached Telchac Puerto, it was surrounded by the Mexican Navy.

"*¡VÁYASE!*" came a voice through a loudspeaker. "*¡RÁPIDO!*" (That means "Get moving—fast!" in Spanish.)

These guys had guns.

Cap'm Duffy had no choice. He turned his little tugboat around and, schlumped across the wheel, he headed back out to sea.

"Where next?" the captain asked Mr. Stroffolino.

"Belize," said Mr. Stroffolino. "It's a country. Next to Mexico. I know dis guy—Rico D'Amico."

BELIZE

LAND OF BANANAS, OF BEAUTIFUL CORAL REEFS,
TROPICAL FLOWERS, AND COLORFUL BIRDS . . .

Pictures of the Garbage Barge had been on the local news. Cap'm Duffy had almost reached the dock when he saw a line of soldiers waving their arms.

"*KUNGO!*" they shouted. (Roughly translated, that means "Fuhgeddaboudit!")

Six weeks had passed since the Garbage Barge had set out, and the garbage was getting REALLY FUNKY. Nobody wanted it. And of course they didn't! It was somebody else's six-week-old garbage!

Cap'm Duffy radioed Mr. Stroffolino once again.

"I can't take it anymore!

I quit!"

"Okay, okay," said Mr. Stroffolino.
"Take da garbage back to Long Island.
But I gotta coupla places you could try
along da way."

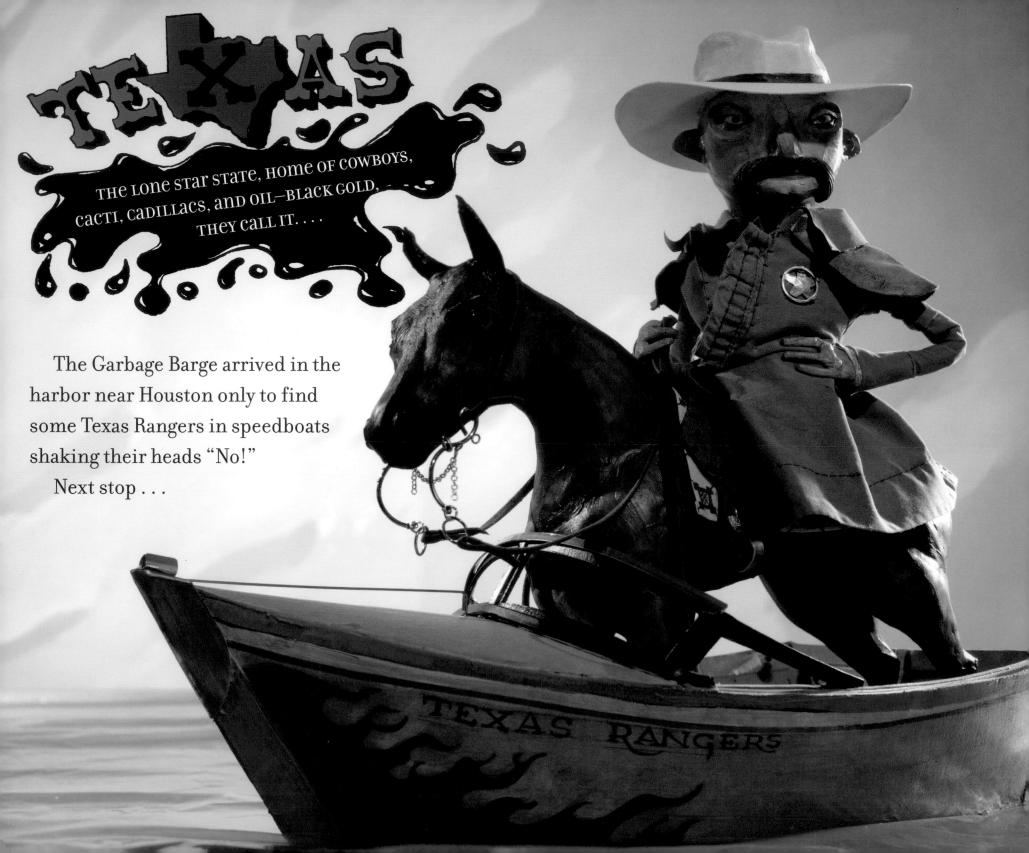

TEXAS

THE LONE STAR STATE, HOME OF COWBOYS, CACTI, CADILLACS, AND OIL—BLACK GOLD, THEY CALL IT. . . .

The Garbage Barge arrived in the harbor near Houston only to find some Texas Rangers in speedboats shaking their heads "No!"

Next stop . . .

TEXAS RANGERS

By now, the Garbage Barge was famous. It had been on TV and in the headlines of all the papers. Comedians even told jokes about it. But as Cap'm Duffy and the *Break of Dawn* tugged it into New York Harbor, they were a sad sight. Cap'm Duffy's mouth hung open. The little tugboat forgot to toot. And the Garbage Barge looked the saddest—and smelled the smelliest—of all.

"Well, me mateys, here we are, back where we began," Cap'm Duffy sighed to his two boats as they finally pulled into Islip's harbor.

But guess what? Islip had seen this coming. They refused to take the garbage.

And the garbage was not welcome anywhere on Long Island or in New Jersey or in New York City, either.

For a whole summer, Cap'm Duffy and his little tugboat tugged the garbage around New York. What else could they do?

"Look, Mom!"

kids would say.

"Here comes the Garbage Barge!"

As the summer days got hotter, the garbage grew beyond stinky. Someone had to take it—they just *had* to.

Then, at last . . .

"Good news!" said Gino Stroffolino when he radioed the tired old captain. "Here's da deal: Brooklyn's gonna take dat garbage and burn it. A judge told 'em dey had to. See, dey got dis 'incinerator.'"

"Aye-aye," mumbled Cap'm Duffy.

And on September 1, 1987, 162 days after the Garbage Barge had first set out, it reached its final harbor.

Brooklyn

Former home of the Dodgers, current home of synagogues and mosques and greasy diners with breakfast specials . . .

BROOKLYN

ENTER

Three thousand one hundred sixty-eight tons of garbage was
unloaded by cranes, put onto trucks, and hauled to the incinerator.
It burned for hours, and when it was done, it only weighed . . .
430 tons.

Then it was hauled off and buried in a landfill in Islip.
The town had been forced by the judge to take back what was left
of its stinking garbage.

Justice!

The *Break of Dawn* and Cap'm Duffy were free to go back to New Orleans. As they steered out to sea, people waved and took pictures.

"It's a fair wind and open sea, me hearties!" the crusty old captain shouted, and he patted the tugboat on its wheel.

Together they had traveled over six thousand miles, tugging the unloved Garbage Barge. It was time to go home.